現代邦楽の父 宮城道雄

千葉優子／文　吉澤みか／絵

《春の海》という曲を知っていますか？　お正月になると必ず耳にする、箏と尺八によるあの音楽です。曲名を知らなくても、聴けばわかります。日本と西洋の音楽を融合した現代の日本音楽です。そして、この《春の海》を作曲したのが宮城道雄でした。

エキゾチックな町、神戸

　1894年4月7日、道雄は菅国治郎とアサ夫妻の長男・菅道雄として、神戸に生まれました。

　6歳年上の姉がおり、2年後には弟が生まれたのですが、その少し後、道雄が4歳の頃に最初の悲しい出来事が起こりました。父との不仲がもとで、母が幼い子どもたちを残して家を出て行ってしまったのです。二人は離婚し、その後、父が再婚したため、道雄はおもに祖母のミネに育てられることになりました。

　道雄は、父が外国人の経営する会社に勤めていたため、「居留地」という外国人が自由に住み、活動することを許されたところに生まれました。ここ居留地には大きな西洋館が建ち並び、並木道を西洋の紳士が裾の長い服を着た女性と外国の言葉を話しながら歩いていきます。ホテルからは西洋の音楽が流れ、時にはオルガンの音も聴こえてきて、日本でありながら別世界のようでした。幼い道雄は、そうしたエキゾチックな雰囲気に包まれて育ってゆくのでした。

居留地の並木道を歩く西洋人の紳士淑女。道沿いには立派な建物がたち、街灯の光が美しく輝いている。

うすれゆく光

　道雄は生後200日頃に眼の病気にかかりました。なんの病気だったのかは、今となってはわかりませんが、父の勤めていた会社の人が赤ん坊の道雄をあやしながら「どうもこの子は目が悪い」と言うのです。

　両親や祖母も心配して、有名な眼医者にもかかりました。その甲斐あってか、一時は少し良くなって、6歳頃までは見えていましたが、次第に悪くなっていきました。

　春になり、道雄のもとにも小学校入学の通知が届き、道雄も期待に胸をふくらませましたが、目が悪かったので、その年は入学を見送りました。来年になれば目が良くなって学校へ行けると楽しみにして、いつでも行けるようにと親たちにいろいろな学用品を買いそろえてもらいました。また、本に目をくっつけるようにして字を習ったり、買ってもらったカバン

校門の前で泣きじゃくる道雄。その肩には、祖母の手がやさしくそえられている。

をかけて学校へ行くまねをして一人で遊んだりもしました。でも、翌年になっても目はいっこうに良くならないばかりか、ますます悪くなる一方でした。

「いつになったらこの目は治るのだろう」

道雄は子ども心にそればかり考えていました。

祖母に手を引かれて、学校の門までよく遊びに行きました。なかから子どもたちが元気に遊び、体操をし、時には歌を歌いながら遠足に出かけるようすが聞こえてきます。ある時、それを聞いていた道雄は急に悲しくなり、門につかまって泣きだしてしまいました。

それでも人一倍負けん気の強かった道雄は目をこすりつけるようにしてカタカナ、ひらがな、そして漢字を習っていましたが、字を書いていると、その字がやがてピンピンと踊るように動きだし、それが最後でだんだんと見えなくなっていきました。

箏の道へ

　8歳の頃、東京からたいへん偉い眼医者が来たというので、道雄は祖母に連れられて病院に行きました。親戚の子どもたちも、「今度は道っちゃんの目が治る」と言って病院の外までついてきました。診察を終えた医者が祖母に向かって告げます。

　「だめだ。どうしても治らない。これからはどんなに良い医者が来ても、また、どんなに良い薬があると言われても、決して迷ってはいけない。それよりもこの子の将来を考えて、何か身につけてやったほうがよかろう」

　道雄の小さな胸はもういっぱいになってしまいました。今日こそ目が治ると思って、楽しみにしてきたのに……。

　門の外で待っていた子どもたち

病院から泣きながら出てきた道雄の顔を、心配そうにのぞきこむ子どもたち。

は、泣きながら祖母に手を引かれて出てきた道雄を取りかこむようにして、

「道っちゃん、目があいたか、目があいたか、見せろ、見せろ」
と言って、やたらに泣いている道雄の顔をのぞきこむのです。それがなおのことつらくて、悲しくて、道雄はますます泣きじゃくるのでした。

医者から失明の宣告を受けた道雄は、箏の道を選ぶことになりました。箏の音楽である「箏曲」と三味線音楽の一つである「地歌」は、江戸時代に盲人男性だけが師匠となることを許された音楽で、この制度がなくなった明治以後も、盲人の重要な職業の一つだったからです。

8歳の道雄は、生田流の二代目中島検校に入門しました。初めての日、高齢の師匠とその夫人は、「よく来た、よく来た」と言って、幼い道雄を引っ張り上げるようにして玄関に上げてくれるのでした。

厳しい修業

道雄が入門してから1年10か月ほど過ぎた頃、二代目中島検校は亡くなり、三代目中島検校に改めて入門しました。

この師匠はたいへんに厳しく、「盲人は記憶力が良くなくてはならん。わしは一度しか教えてやらんから、一度習ったことを忘れないように」と弟子に厳しく注意しました。

《娘道成寺》という曲を習っているときのことです。道雄は「諸行無常」「是生滅法」「生滅滅已」「寂滅為楽」という歌詞がどうしても覚えられなくて、苦にしていました。それを見かねた祖母が

「もう一度教わりに行こう。もし叱られたら自分が先生によく頼んでやるから」

と言って、夜道を二人で師匠の家へ向かいました。道雄は手を引かれながら、師匠に叱られることを覚悟するのでした。

ところが、師匠は「よく来た」と道雄を迎え、「お前は意味がわからんから、覚えられないのだ」と言って、その意味をよく教えてくれました。それがまた難しくて、聞いていてもやっぱりよくわかりません。それでも道雄は、今度こそ意味だけは必ず覚えて帰ろうと思うのでした。

また、寒稽古といって、最も寒い時期の早朝に冷たい風の吹きすさぶなかで稽古することもありました。難しい曲を、百篇、千篇と繰り返し弾き、冷たくて手の感覚がなくなると、金だらいの氷の張った水に手をつけてから、また弾き始め、しまいには指から血が出ることもありました。

こうして寒稽古はほぼ1か月続けられました。肉体的にもかなり過酷な修業でしたが、道雄は最後まで成し遂げるのでした。

厳しい寒さに耐えながら、箏の稽古を続ける道雄。

免許皆伝

　厳しい修業の甲斐あって、道雄の腕はめきめき上達しましたが、道雄はまたしても不運に見舞われます。

　1905年、道雄が11歳の年のことです。父の国治郎は、それまで勤めていた会社をやめて、独立して事業を営んでいましたが、その事業に失敗し、道雄と祖母を日本に残して、家族で朝鮮（現韓国）に渡って雑貨商を営んでいました。ところが、運悪く暴動に巻きこまれて商品すべてを略奪されたうえに重傷を負って働けなくなり、道雄に仕送りをすることもできなくなってしまったのです。

　道雄は祖母と一緒に、師匠のもとへ相談に行きました。同情した師匠は、道雄の収入源となるように、助手に取り立ててくれることになりました。でも、それには道雄が免許皆伝となる必要があります。そのためには高額な謝礼を支

払わなければなりません。もちろん、道雄がそのような支払いなどできるはずもなく、子ども心に悩んでいると、師匠はいつもより低い声で、「お前は家庭の事情で免状のお金は出せないのだろうが、それでは皆の手前、お前も心苦しいだろう。そのお金は私が立て替

免許皆伝に必要なお金を立て替えることを提案する師匠の前で、ただただ涙を流す道雄。

えて出しておいてやるから、お前はほかの者と一緒に自分で持ってきたようにして納めるのがよいであろう」と言うのでした。

道雄は師匠の温情に胸がいっぱいになり、お礼を言うにも言葉にならず、ただただ涙ばかりがとめどもなく流れるのでした。のちに

道雄は「師匠の恩のありがたいことを忘れることができない」と語っています。

1905年、晴れて免許皆伝となった道雄は、師匠の中島の「中」の字を許されて、芸名「中菅道雄」となるのでした。

朝鮮へ

　ある日、まだ傷の治っていない父が朝鮮から道雄を訪ねてきました。

　「どうしても道雄の助けが必要だ」と言うのです。

　今ようやく自分だけは何とか生活ができるようになった道雄でしたが、今度は朝鮮へ行って、一家を支えなければなりません。まだ習っていない曲もある修業中の身でしたが、敬愛する師匠のもとを離れ、遠い見知らぬ朝鮮の地へ旅立つのでした。13歳の夏のことです。

　1907年９月、道雄は祖母と共に京城（現ソウル）から西へ45キロほどの港町、仁川（現インチョン）に渡りました。道雄たち家族みんなが住んだ家は、六畳と四畳半の２間という小さな家でした。昼間は女性の弟子たちに箏を教え、夜は自己流で覚えた尺八を「おじさんたち」に教えて、道雄は一家の生計を支えました。

　自分自身の勉強をもっとしたいと思っていた道雄は、いつも朝早くみんながまだ寝ているうちから起きて、一人で箏の練習をしていました。そのせいか、夜になると日中の疲れが出て、尺八を教えながらどうしても居眠りをしてしまいます。とうとう弟子たちが怒って来なくなってしまい、父と一緒に謝りに行ったこともありました。

　それでも、少年の身では、どんなに一生懸命に箏や尺八を教えても、一家を充分に養うことはできません。この頃いちばんつらかったのは、父が借金取りに謝っているのを聞くことでした。とはいえ、貧しかったせいか、むしろ一家の気持ちは家族的であったといいます。

尺八を教えながら弟子の前で居眠りをしてしまう道雄。

最初の作品《水の変態》

　朝鮮に住むようになってからは、あいにく教わる先生もなく、すでに習った曲ばかり練習していた道雄は、何か飽き足らないものを感じて、作曲をしてみたいと考えるようになりました。

　ある日、高等小学2年（現在の小学6年）の弟・啓二が、教科書に載っていた「水の変態」を読んでいるのを聞いて、道雄は、ふとひかれるものを感じました。それは、水が霧、雲、雨、雪、霰、露、そして霜になる、その千変万化を表わした和歌7首です。

　道雄の住んでいた古びた家の軒から落ちる雫の音、トタン屋根を打つリズミカルな雨音、雨から雪に降り変わる音、霰の音、シトシトと落ちる雪解けの雫。これらの音を常日頃から興味深く聞いていた道雄は、弟の読む「水の変態」に表わされた自然の妙が手にとるように実感できたのです。

　「ぜひ、これに曲をつけてみたい」

　それからというもの、毎日、弾いては直し、弾いては直し、かれこれ30日ばかりして、ようやく自分でも納得のゆくものになりました。曲想を練り、作曲に苦心する日々の楽しかったこと。それ以来、道雄は作曲にとても興味を覚えたのです。

道雄の頭のなかに、《水の変態》のイメージが広がる。

　この曲こそ道雄の最初の作品であり、彼の四百数十曲に及ぶ作品のなかでも屈指の名曲である《水の変態》です。1909年、14歳の頃に作曲された、演奏時間が17分ほどかかるこの大曲は、日本の音楽史に輝かしい1ページを書き加えました。

　この年の夏、仁川に立ち寄った当時統監だった伊藤博文は、道雄の演奏する《水の変態》を聴いて、「少年ながら見事だ。必ずお前を東京へ連れて帰ろう」と語りました。けれども、その3か月余り後、伊藤はハルビンの駅頭で狙撃され帰らぬ人となり、この瞬間、道雄の希望は霧と散じ露と消えるのでした。

中菅から宮城へ

　1910年、《水の変態》を作曲した翌年に、道雄の世話をしていた祖母が風邪をこじらせて亡くなり、父もその頃から役所に勤めるようになったため、道雄は家族のもとを離れて朝鮮の中心都市である京城にいた弟子の小西マスの家で暮らすことになりました。小西夫妻は、以前から菅家を経済的に援助していたのです。

　天才少年箏曲家、中菅道雄は李王妃殿下の御前演奏を依頼されるなど、ますます有名になることで弟子の数も増え、生活にも多少の余裕が出てきました。すると、もっと勉強したいとの思いから、1911年7月に弟の啓二に付き添われて旧師中島検校のもとへ行き、約1か月のあいだ泊まりこんで、まだ習っていない曲の習得に努めました。啓二の中学校の夏休みを利用してのことです。

　やがて、小西夫妻は啓二の養育費と学費を引き受けるので、小西夫人の親戚である喜多仲子という箏曲地歌の演奏をする未亡人と道雄が結婚して、夫婦養子の形で、当時絶えていた仲子の実家である宮城家を再興してほしいという申し出を道雄の父にしました。そし

長谷幸輝大検校による地歌三味線の演奏に耳を傾ける、道雄とその妻・仲子。

て、道雄は仲子と結婚し、「宮城道雄」という名前が誕生するのでした。

1913年12月28日からは、仲子の付き添いで道雄は70日間にも及ぶ日本での修業の旅に出ました。神戸では、熊本の地歌三味線の名人、長谷幸輝大検校の演奏にも触れ、道雄にとっては実り多い旅となりました。

このように、道雄は朝鮮時代も進んで古典音楽の修業をしました。日本で自分の作品を発表したときには「古典を知らぬ宮城」と批判されることもありましたが、実際は古典をこよなく愛し、その修業にも精進していたのです。

上京に向けての出会い

　1916年には22歳の若さで「大検校」という箏曲地歌界の最高位へと上りつめ、名実ともに朝鮮箏曲界の覇者となった道雄でしたが、それに満足することなく、日本一をめざして、何としても東京に出て自らの作品を世に問いたいと考えるようになりました。そして、道雄の上京を後押しする人々との出会いもありました。

　後年、道雄との名コンビで「新日本音楽運動」（→p22）を展開した尺八家の吉田晴風との出会いも、1914年6月、京城でのことでした。箏曲地歌は、明治以後からは尺八と合奏することが多かったのです。道雄より3歳年上の晴風は、「時が来れば君を迎えに来るから」と言い残して、翌1915年9月、東京へと旅立ちました。

　この年の10月には、都山流尺八の創始者、中尾都山との出会いもありました。翌年再び京城に

尺八を吹く吉田晴風と、三味線を弾く道雄。

やってきた都山は、道雄作曲の箏と三味線の四重奏曲《唐砧》の斬新さに胸うたれ、さらに道雄の三味線の腕前にも感心するのでした。

そのひと月後、今度は琴古流尺八の大御所、川瀬順輔と、その夫人で長谷大検校（→P17）の筆頭弟子であり東京の箏曲地歌界に多大な影響を及ぼした里子は、道雄の才能を見抜いて上京を勧めました。

道雄は、まるで上京のための総仕上げをするかのように、12月26日から、熊本の長谷大検校のもとへ稽古に向かいました。その間に、晴風から上京を促す手紙も届いて、道雄は明けて1917年、春まだ浅き2月、約10年に及んで生活してきた朝鮮を後にするのでした。

第1回作品発表会の衝撃

　1917年4月、東京駅のプラットホームに降り立った道雄は、「来たな！」という吉田晴風の大きな声にほっとしました。

　晴風の借家に身を寄せ、その後、川瀬夫妻の世話で小さな家を借りて「箏曲教授」の看板を出しましたが、なかなか弟子は集まりません。朝鮮で不動の地位を築いていた道雄でしたが、ここ東京では全く無名の新人にすぎなかったからです。

　道雄が初めて東京で注目されたのは、1919年5月に本郷の中央会堂で開かれた第1回目の作品発表会でした。東京駅に降り立ってから2年、25歳の時でした。

　この演奏会までの生活は、貧困や妻・仲子の病死など惨憺たるものでした。それが、こうして作品発表会を開くことができたのは、吉田晴風をはじめとする支援者、そして1918年に再婚した貞子の

第1回目の作品発表会で箏を弾く道雄。背景には、本郷の中央会堂の建物が描かれている。

おかげでした。

　第1回作品発表会で演奏されたのは全部で11曲。《水の変態》や《唐砧》など、すべての作品が従来の箏曲地歌の概念からは大きく逸脱した道雄の個性あふれる作品のみで構成されていました。

　そして、その評価は大きく二つに分かれたのです。総じて洋楽家や学者、文学者は好意を示しましたが、邦楽家たちの多くは反感を持ちました。

　「箏曲の伝統を破壊し、いたずらに奇をてらうものだ」
　と異端視され、

　「あれは古典を知らないからだ」
　と酷評されたのです。

　一方、単なる西洋音楽の技法の消化にとどまらず、邦楽の要素や手法を取り入れようと意識的に努力しだしていた洋楽界の人々は、道雄の作品に注目しました。

「新日本音楽」の誕生

　翌1920年11月27日に、道雄は洋楽系作曲家の本居長世と合同作品発表会「新日本音楽大演奏会」を開催しました。

　本居は《七つの子》や《赤い靴》などの童謡の作曲家として今は有名ですが、当時は童謡だけではなく、邦楽の要素を取り入れた洋楽の作曲をめざしていました。そこで、洋楽の要素を取り入れた邦楽を作曲していた道雄と合同の演奏会を開き、大評判となったのです。ただし、本居は次第に童謡や歌曲などを主に作曲するようになり、「新日本音楽」の名称も使わなくなりました。

　一方、邦楽界では道雄の活動に追随する者も現れてきましたが、彼らの作品は「箏曲地歌」や「尺八楽」などといった従来のジャンル名ではもはや分類できなかったため、放送やレコード、演奏会プログラムの曲目分類として「新日本音楽」の名称が使われました。やがて、この名称は、道雄を中心とした大正から昭和初期にかけての邦楽近代化をめざした音楽活動、またその作品を指す歴史的用語として定着したのです。

　それらの音楽的特徴は、西洋音楽を意識して作曲された日本の伝統楽器を主体とした音楽、つまり、邦楽に西洋音楽の要素を導入して、時代に即した新しい音楽を創ろうとしたものでした。

山間に日が沈み、夕焼けの空にカラスが飛んでいる様子を背景に立つ本居長世。手前には、日本の伝統音楽の改革をめざす宮城道雄がいる。

和洋の融合

　道雄は幼少期に神戸の居留地で西洋音楽を聴きながら育ちました。朝鮮では、駐屯していた日本の軍楽隊や、レコードを聴かせてくれたギリシャ人との交流で、いっそう西洋音楽に興味を持つようになりましたが、本格的に西洋音楽の勉強を始めたのは、1917年に東京へ来てからです。

　音楽学者の田辺尚雄の講義を聞き、チェロのシコラやヴァイオリンのハイフェッツなど来日中の一流演奏家の音楽会にも行きました。

　外国から西洋音楽の点字楽譜*を取り寄せて研究し、道雄自身が「レコードは先生である」と語るように、レコードでも勉強しました。こうして独学で西洋音楽を学び、その要素を邦楽に取り入れたのです。

　有名な《春の海》も形式はA-B-A′という西洋の三部形式で

す。美しく覚えやすい旋律もリズムも西洋的なもので、これらは日本の伝統的な箏曲地歌の旋律やリズムとは異なります。その一方で、日本の伝統的な音階を使うなどして日本らしさを醸し出しています。そのため、ピアノやフルートなど西洋の楽器で演奏しても日本的ですし、現代の日本人が、必ず日本音楽の代表として挙げる音楽です。そして、この曲は外国の人にもわかりやすい日本の音楽なのです。

　逆に、《水の変態》は、音階も形式もリズムも旋律もすべて伝統的ですが、しかし、作曲の根本である創作姿勢、作曲態度そのものが革新的でした。というのは、従来の箏曲が類型的な音型や旋律の組み合わせによって作曲するため、抽象的で感情を抑えた音楽だったのに対して、《水の変態》では独創的な旋律や音型を豊富に

用いて、情景描写に努力を払った個性的な作品となっていたからです。この「個性」を重視した作曲が従来の邦楽とは異なり、いわば西洋の近代的な作曲姿勢にも通ず

るもので、現在高く評価されるゆえんなのです。

＊指先の触覚でわかるように、音の高さや長さなどを突起した6つの点の組み合わせであらわした楽譜。

心を描く《春の海》

　《春の海》は1929年の暮れに、翌年の歌会始の勅題「海辺の巌」に因んで作曲され、1930年1月2日に広島放送局から放送初演されました。今でこそ、道雄の最も有名な作品となっていますが、発表当初は、さほど評判になりませんでした。

　それを一躍有名にしたのが、フランスの女性ヴァイオリン奏者、ルネ・シュメーとの合奏です。シュメーは日本の音楽を聴くために道雄のもとを訪れ、《春の海》をとても気に入って、自ら尺八パートをヴァイオリンに編曲し、1932年5月31日の「シュメー告別演奏会」で道雄と演奏したのです。それが大評判となり、二人でレコーディングをして日本・フランス・アメリカから発売され、好評

フランスのヴァイオリニスト、ルネ・シュメーと《春の海》を合奏する道雄。背景には、春の海のイメージが描かれている。

を博して、「宮城道雄」の名が世界に知られるようになりました。

道雄は作曲の動機を「かつて瀬戸内海を船で通った折に、春ののどかな雰囲気を心に感じて作曲した」と随筆に記しています。

道雄はよく自然から曲想を得て作曲します。道雄の音楽の特徴の一つに描写性がありますが、それは擬音や擬声などの具体的な音の描写ではなく、漠然と心に描いた印象を音楽的に表現するものでし

た。目の見えない道雄の作品を聴いて、私たちはその情景を思い描くことができます。このようなイメージ描写の世界は、道雄が大好きだったラヴェルやドビュッシーなど近代フランス音楽に通じるものでもあります。《春の海》のゆったりとした旋律も、道雄が春の海に対して持つイメージを心に感じた結果で、そうした心の動きを描いているからこそ、人々の心に直接訴えてくるのです。

随筆と音楽

　宮城道雄というと、目が見えず、幼くして母と生き別れ、極貧の生活をした生い立ちなどから暗い印象を持たれがちですが、その素顔は実に人間味にあふれていました。にぎやかなことが好きで、冗談が好きで、雷が大っ嫌いな、茶目っ気たっぷりの明るい人柄は、彼の随筆に垣間見ることができます。

　1935年、親友で随筆家の内田百閒の勧めで最初の随筆集『雨の念仏』を出版して以来、生前に7タイトルの随筆集を出版し、川端康成や室生犀星ら一流の文学者はじめ、各界から高く評価されました。

　音楽家として功成り名を遂げた人物の随筆であるにもかかわらず、大家らしい逸話も大仰な芸談もありません。むしろ失敗談を明るく描いています。まわりの人々に対する感謝の気持ちや、自然を愛でるものが多く、随所に彼一流のウィットに富んだ表現が見られます。また、悲しいこと、つらいことを書く時も激することなく実に淡々と記され、それゆえに、かえって読む者の胸に迫ります。

　目の見えた幼い頃の思い出は実に視覚的に鮮やかに描かれますが、見えなくなると、視覚的表現はまったく影をひそめます。しかし、ここから道雄の鋭い感性とユニークな視点による独自の世界が展開されるのです。聴覚や触覚などの感覚すべてを使って、自然の素晴らしさを感受性豊かに描き、文学的に彼独自のスタイルを創り上げました。

　これらは視覚を失った道雄の感性のあらわれであると同時に、《水の変態》や《春の海》など、自然をテーマに数多くの作曲をおこなった彼の音楽作品にも一脈通じるものなのです。

点字タイプライターを打って、随筆を書く道雄。

新楽器の開発

　道雄は新様式の音楽をつくるために、新しく楽器も開発しました。

　最初の新楽器は1921年10月の演奏会で発表された「十七絃」です。この楽器は低い音を出すための大型の箏で、今や完全に日本の楽器として定着して、現在も多くの作曲家がこの楽器を使った音楽を作曲しています。

　1925年頃には、従来の胡弓の音量を増やして、低い音も出るように音域を広げた大型の胡弓も開発しました。現在、「大胡弓」あるいは「宮城胡弓」といわれているものです（→P33）。

　そして、1929年11月の演奏会では、80本の弦を張ったグランドピアノのような形の箏「八十絃」を発表しました。箏の音色と特性を尊重し

グランドピアノのように大きい「八十絃」を弾く道雄。

つつ、音域を広げようとした楽器です。けれども、80本もの弦に対して共鳴板の役割を担う胴が小さすぎたため、音響的にも失敗して、結局、戦火に消えてしまいました。

やがて1955年頃から、さまざまな箏曲家らによって「三十絃」や「二十絃箏」「二十五絃箏」などが開発されましたが、八十絃はこうした多絃箏の先駆けといえるかもしれません。

また、1932年には、箏の簡便化と大衆化を図って、従来の箏の三分の二程度と短く、素人でも簡単に弦を締めることができるようにネジを使った「短琴」をつくりました。これは、他の新楽器と違って学校での使用を考えてのものです。

このように、道雄は教育活動にも熱心でした。

教授法の改革と童曲

　従来の教授法と大きく異なる道雄の教授法の一つが、楽譜を積極的に活用したことです。これまでは楽譜を使わなかったために、曲を覚えるのに多くの時間が費やされました。けれども、道雄は楽譜を使うことで、むしろ、その先のテクニックや音楽創りなどを主に教育し、教授法を合理化したのです。これは道雄自身が楽譜の利便性をよく知っていたからのことでしょう。道雄は14、5歳の頃、すでに点字を習っていて、点字楽譜を早くから使っていたのです。

　1930年８月にはラジオ放送による箏曲講習もおこない、好評を博しました。そのため、数度にわたり放送されましたが、毎回、テキストを作成しました。これをもとに、全くの初心者が箏曲地歌の演奏技法を習得できるようにつくられたのが、『宮城道雄小曲集』という完成度の高い教則本でし

た。歌のない小曲と歌のある小曲を段階的に配置して難度を上げていくのですが、その際、「童曲」を使いました。童曲とは、道雄が上京当初から童謡詩人の葛原しげるとともにつくっていた子どものための箏曲です。歌詞を覚えるのに苦労した自らの経験に基づくのかもしれません。

　元来、教育は地味な仕事です。作品として残るわけでもなく、演奏のようにスポットライトが当たることもありません。そのうえ、なかなか効果も上がらないのです。それでも、道雄はむしろ進んでこの地味な仕事に力を注ぐのでした。

　さらに、童曲は胡弓で犬や猫の鳴き声を真似るなどして、聴いて楽しい音楽としての工夫もしたので、演奏会やレコードで人気を博し、箏曲人口を増やすことにもなりました。

童曲を歌う子どもの横で、女性が箏を、道雄が大胡弓を弾いている。背景には、『宮城道雄小曲集』の本がイメージとして描かれている。

古典を現代に甦らせる演奏

　演奏においても道雄は新生面を切り開いて、邦楽の近代化をはかり、江戸時代以来の古典曲を現代に甦らせました。

　元来、箏曲地歌は家庭内のお座敷など狭い空間で、教養や娯楽として自ら演奏して楽しむ音楽でした。けれども西洋音楽の影響で音楽自体を純粋に鑑賞するための演奏会が登場することで、お座敷からホールへと演奏の場が移り、それに即した演奏法を道雄は開発したのです。

　まず楽器については、山田流で使われていた装飾のない澄んだ音色の素箏仕立ての箏を生田流の道

箏を弾く道雄の手。

雄も使い、さらに、箏爪を薄くし、弦を細くするなど、さまざまに工夫することで、繊細で芯のある美しい音色が広いホールでも響き渡る演奏を確立しました。

　また、演奏の面では、音楽の流れを重視した推進力のある演奏です。テンポが速いということではありません。「ノリ」のよい演奏で、音楽に内在する強弱法やフレーズ感を捉えて、それを自然に表現するという従来の古典的な演奏法とは異なる演奏によって人々を魅了しました。

　ある洋楽系作曲家は、「古めかしい古典でありながら、宮城の現代人の共感を得る緻密な表現力によって古典の美しさを再発見した」と述べています。

大編成による新様式の音楽

　日本の楽器による合奏曲や合唱合奏曲など多くの楽器を使った大編成の作品も、道雄が開拓した新様式の音楽です。

　箏曲地歌の古典的な編成では、歌と箏・三味線・尺八または胡弓による三曲合奏がいちばん大きな編成でしたが、道雄はさらに大きな編成の作曲をしました。

　このタイプの作品では、道雄自身が開発した十七絃が低音部を支える楽器として、また、大胡弓が旋律を奏でる楽器として使用されたばかりでなく、雅楽の楽器である笙・鞨鼓・楽太鼓、また囃子の楽器である小鼓、さらには西洋の楽器であるフルートなど、必要な音色を得るために洋の東西を問わず、あらゆる楽器を自由に使って大編成の合奏曲や合唱合奏曲を作曲したのです。

　元来、日本の伝統的な音楽では

ステージで箏とオーケストラによる協奏曲が演奏されている様子。

雅楽、長唄、能など、それぞれのジャンルによって使う楽器が異なっていました。笙や鞨鼓は雅楽でしか使いませんし、三味線は雅楽や能では使いません。けれども、道雄はこうした垣根を取り払い、さまざまな楽器を自由に使うことによって、それまでの日本の音楽にはなかった新しい編成による新しい音楽を創り出したのです。作曲に際して、道雄はすでに音楽のイメージがあって、それを具現化する音色を得るために、楽器を自由に使いました。

また、1928年に昭和天皇の即位を祝う音楽として依頼されて作曲した《越天楽変奏曲》をはじめとして、4曲の箏と西洋のオーケストラによる協奏曲も洋楽系作曲家と共作しました。そして、これら大編成の音楽には道雄が教授を務めていた東京音楽学校（現東京藝術大学音楽学部）などに依頼されて作曲したものが多く、当時、こうした音楽が高く評価されていたことがうかがえます。

突然の死と永遠の命

　第二次世界大戦後、道雄の人気はますます高まっていきました。終戦からわずか半年後の1946年2月には歌舞伎の音楽を担当するなど、歌舞伎や映画、舞踊の音楽をはじめ多くの作曲を依頼されました。また戦後の民放各局の開設に伴いラジオ出演も増え、レギュラー番組も抱えるなか、全国各地での演奏会、そして東京藝術大学等での教授活動もおこない、多忙をきわめていました。

　そんななか、国際民族音楽協会（現国際伝統音楽協会）主催の会議や演奏会に日本代表として参加するための渡欧の依頼も舞い込みました。1953年夏、道雄は43日間に及ぶ演奏旅行へと赴き、スペインのパンプロナでの演奏会で第1位となるなど、大きな成果を残して帰国するのでした。

　1956年6月24日、道雄は関西交響楽団と《越天楽変奏曲》を共演するために、寝台急行「銀河」に姪の喜代子とともに乗車していました。大阪、神戸、京都と巡演するもので、関西でのオーケストラとの大々的な演奏会に、かなり乗り気だったといいます。

　列車が動き出すと、道雄は読書を始め、いつものように日本酒を飲みながら喜代子と話をし、2度ほどトイレへ連れて行ってもらいました。11時頃、喜代子は、「トイレの時は私を起こしてください」と、念を押して眠りにつきました。

　ところが、翌25日未明のことです。道雄は刈谷駅から東へ500メートルほどのガード下あたりで列車から転落しているところを発見されました。駅員によって病院

に運ばれる途中、「ここはどこですか？」と尋ねるなど言葉を交わし、病院で処置を受けたのですが、次第に意識が遠のき、午前7時15分、道雄は人気絶頂のさなか、誰一人知る者もない旅先の病室で、62年の生涯を閉じるのでした。

NHK（エヌエイチケイ）は朝のニュースで道雄の悲報を伝え、この日の夕刊各紙が写真入りで大きく報じました。あまりに突然の死に、日本中の人々が、衝撃を受けるのでした。

けれども、今なお道雄の創り出した《春の海》はじめ多くの作品が演奏され続けています。そればかりか、彼の開発した楽器や作曲法がなければ、今の日本の音楽シーンは生まれませんでした。

宮城道雄は、自ら生み出した音楽のなかで永遠に生き続けてゆくことでしょう。

光に向かって走る寝台急行「銀河」と宮城道雄。道雄の音楽が生き続けることをイメージして描かれている。

読者のみなさまへ

　本書は、今から130年前の明治時代、日清戦争の折に、兵庫県の神戸で誕生した視覚障害のある偉人「宮城道雄」の一生をもとにつくられた絵本です。

　道雄は22歳の若さで「大検校」となり、箏曲地歌界の最高位に昇り詰めた人です。生後200日で目の病気にかかり、8歳の頃に眼医者の先生から失明宣告を受けました。先生は道雄の将来を考え、何か身につくものをやった方がよかろうと祖母に助言。そのことがきっかけとなり、道雄は箏の道を選びました。

　良き師匠に出会い、厳しい修行にも耐え、道雄の箏の腕はめきめき上達しました。師匠の教えのなかで、「盲人は記憶力が良くなくてはならない。わしは一度しか教えてやらんから、一度習ったことを忘れないように」と厳しく注意を与えられたことは、道雄の糧となりました。寒稽古も厳しいものでしたが、最後まで成し遂げ、道雄は11歳で免許皆伝。「師匠の恩のありがたいことを忘れることはできない」と、彼が残した言葉が印象的です。

　さらに、道雄が14歳の時のこと。弟が教科書にある和歌「水の変態」を朗読しており、水が霧、雲、雨、雪、霰、露そして霜になる千変万化の7首を聞いていました。音に関する感性が人一倍優れている道雄は、弟の読んでいる水の変態を実感し、曲にしました。それが、最初の作曲となる「水の変態」です。これを機に、道雄は曲づくりにも興味を覚えたのでした。

　22歳の若さで「大検校」となり、箏曲地歌界の最高位に上り詰めたころから、道雄には日本一の奏者を目指して東京に出たい思いが募りました。念願が叶い、23歳の春から東京での生活をスタートした道雄は、邦楽近代化を目指した音楽活動「新日本音楽」の名称を発表会に使いました。しかしこの名称は邦楽に西洋音楽の要素を取り入れたものだということもあり、当初は邦楽家からの反感も見られました。

　評価を2分するなかでつくられた曲が「春の海」でした。歌会始の勅題「海辺の巌」に因んだもので、道雄が心に描いた印象を音楽で表現したものです。自然の素晴らしさを感性豊かに描き、独自のスタイルをつくりあげたのです。この曲は日本、フランス、アメリカで発売され、やがては世界中で知られるようになりました。ヘレン・ケラー初来日の折には、日比谷公会堂で「春の海」の箏演奏を行い、ヘレンと道雄は心と心での親交を深めたのでした。

　絵本の作成は、文では千葉優子さまの巧みな文体により、宮城道雄の世界をわかりやすく表現してもらいました。日本画家の吉澤みかさまの描かれた箏を奏でる絵は、メロディーが浮かんでくるようです。

　本書の発行にあたり、小学館、一般財団法人日本児童教育振興財団より、ご支援を賜わりましたことに厚く御礼申し上げます。また、この絵本の製作に関わっていただいた全ての方々に、当会を代表して深く御礼申し上げます。

2024年12月
社会福祉法人　桜雲会　理事長　一幡良利

文／千葉優子

武蔵野音楽大学大学院修士課程終了（音楽学専攻）。現在、一般財団法人宮城道雄記念館資料室室長。『筆を友として―評伝宮城道雄』（2015 アルテスパブリッシング）で第28回ミュージック・ペンクラブ音楽賞、『ドレミを選んだ日本人』（2007 音楽之友社）で第23回ヨゼフ・ロゲンドルフ賞を受賞。『箏曲の歴史入門』『日本音楽がわかる本』（以上、音楽之友社）ほか著書論文多数。「宮城道雄の世界」（NHKラジオ第2にて26回放送）など放送講演活動もおこなう。

絵／吉澤みか

1963年京都府生まれ。日本画家。京都精華大学美術学部造形学科日本画専攻卒業。京都市立芸術大学美術学部大学院修了。京都美術展（奨励賞受賞）、京展ほか入選多数。大人も読める絵本『ざっそう weeds』『駅のピアノ　故国への想い』（ともに今人舎）の絵を担当。

英訳／ノビ・キーリ（Nobby Kealey）

1957年イギリス・マンチェスター生まれ。シェフィールド大学にて日本語を専攻。来日後はカメラマンとして活躍する一方、英語教師のほか、数々のテレビCMに出演。現在、錦城高等学校英語講師。

監修／社会福祉法人　桜雲会

1892年、東京盲唖学校（現在の筑波大学附属視覚特別支援学校）の生徒の同窓会として発足。1930年に最初の鍼按科教科書を出版。以後、医学専門書を中心に点字図書や録音図書、拡大図書の製作・販売をおこなう。

資料提供／一般財団法人　宮城道雄記念館

編集・デザイン・DTP制作／
　　株式会社 今人舎（二宮祐子／矢野瑛子）

現代邦楽の父 宮城道雄

2025年2月10日 初版発行　　　　　　　　　　　　　　　　NDC289

文	千葉優子	
絵	吉澤みか	
発行者	一幡良利	
発行所	社会福祉法人桜雲会	

　　　　〒169−0075 東京都新宿区高田馬場4−11−14−102
　　　　電話　03−5337−7866　http://ounkai.jp

印刷・製本　株式会社瞬報社

©Yuko Chiba, Mika Yoshizawa 2025, Printed in Japan, Published by Ounkai　　　48P　210 × 260mm
ISBN978-4-911208-10-6

Miyagi Michio
--The Father of Modern Japanese Music

Text: Chiba Yūko   Illustrations: Yoshizawa Mika

P1

Do you know the song *"Haru no Umi"* ("The Sea in Spring")? It's a piece of music performed on the *koto* and *shakuhachi* which you are sure to hear at New Year. Even if you don't know the title, you will recognize it when you hear it. It is a piece of modern Japanese music that fuses Japanese and Western styles. And the composer of *"Haru no Umi"* was Miyagi Michio.

P2-3

The Exotic City of Kobe

Michio was born in Kobe on April 7, 1894 as Suga Michio, the first son of Suga Kunijirō and his wife Asa. He had an older sister, six years his senior, and a younger brother born two years later. However, shortly afterward, when Michio was four years old, the first sad event of his life occurred. Due to disagreements between his parents, his mother left the household, leaving her young children behind. The couple divorced and his father remarried, so Michio was mostly raised by his grandmother, Mine.

As his father worked for a foreign-owned company, when Michio was born they lived in an area called the "settlement" where foreigners were allowed to live and conduct their activities freely. In this settlement, large Western-style mansions lined the streets, and Western gentlemen would walk along tree-lined avenues, speaking in foreign languages to women in long, flowing dresses. Western music played from the hotels, and at times, you could even hear the sound of an organ. It was like a different world, even though it was in Japan. The young Michio grew up surrounded by this exotic atmosphere.

Caption:
A Western gentleman and a lady stroll along a tree-lined avenue in the settlement. Stately mansions stand along the road and the street lamps cast a beautiful, warm glow.

P4-5

Fading Light

When he was about 200 days old, Michio developed an eye disease. It's unclear now what the illness was, but, as one of his father's colleagues was cradling the infant Michio, the man remarked, "This child seems to have poor eyesight."

His parents and grandmother were worried and even took him to a famous eye doctor. Perhaps because of that, Michio's vision improved for a while, and he could still see until he was about six years old. However, his sight was gradually worsening.

When spring arrived, Michio received notice that he would be entering elementary school. He was filled with anticipation, but because of his poor eyesight, it was decided he wouldn't enter that year. Believing his vision would improve, he looked forward to going to school the following year and his parents bought him various school supplies so he could go whenever he wanted to. He practiced reading by holding books close to his face and even played by himself, pretending to go to school carrying the school bag that was bought for him. However, by the following year, not only had his eyesight not improved, it had worsened even further.

"When will my eyes get better?"

This was all the young Michio could think about.

Holding his grandmother's hand, he was often taken for a walk to the school gates. From inside, Michio could hear the lively voices of children having fun, doing exercises and sometimes singing songs as they went off on field trips. One day, as Michio listened to all this, he was suddenly overcome with sadness and, clinging to the school gate, he burst into tears.

Still, he had such a strong desire not to be beaten that he pushed his face ever closer to the paper while learning *katakana*, *hiragana* and *kanji*. But, as he wrote characters on the page, they would soon begin to move and dance before his eyes. Gradually, they disappeared from view and he lost his sight completely.

Caption:
Michio sobs uncontrollably in front of the school gates as his grandmother's hand rests gently on his shoulder.

P6-7

Path to The *Koto*

When Michio was about 8 years old, his grandmother took him to the hospital as a famous eye-doctor was visiting from Tokyo. Some of his cousins went with them to the hospital, saying, "This time Michio's eyes will be cured." After examining Michio, the doctor spoke to his grandmother.

"It's no use. His eyes won't get better. From now on, no matter how good the doctor is, or how good they say the medicine is, you must never be swayed by them. Instead, think about this child's future and help him to learn a skill."

Michio's small heart was overwhelmed. He'd been looking forward to coming here, believing that, today, his eyes would finally be healed.

Michio was crying as he was led out of the hospital by his grandmother. The other children, who had waited outside, surrounded him, asking , "Michio, can you see? Can you see? Show us, show us!" They peered into his tearful face but this only deepened his sadness and he cried even harder.

After hearing from the doctor that he would definitely go blind, Michio decided to learn the *koto*. During the Edo period, only blind men were allowed to become teachers of *koto* music (*sōkyoku*) and a type of *shamisen* music (*jiuta*) and even after the rules changed in the Meiji period, these were still important jobs for blind people.

At the age of eight, Michio became a student of the master Nakajima *Kengyō* II of the Ikuta school of *koto* music. On his first day, the elderly master and his wife greeted the young Michio warmly, saying, "Welcome, welcome," as they helped him up into the house.

Caption:
The children look worriedly at Michio's tear-streaked face as he comes out of the hospital

P8-9

Strict Training

About a year and ten months after Michio began his training, his master passed away. Michio then became a student of his successor, Nakajima *Kengyō* III.

This new master was very strict and warned his apprentices, "A blind person must have a good memory. I will teach you once only, so don't forget what you have learned."

One time, Michio was learning the song "*Musume Dōjōji*", but he struggled to memorize the difficult lyrics: "The impermanence of all things", "This is the law of creation and destruction", "Beyond creation and destruction into Nirvana", "Freedom from desire is bliss". No matter how hard he tried, he couldn't remember them. His grandmother, unable to bear watching him struggle, said, "Let's go and ask the master to teach it again. If he scolds you, I'll plead with him on your behalf." So, the two of them headed to the master's house late at night. Holding on to his grandmother's hand, Michio was prepared for a scolding.

However, when they arrived, the master welcomed Michio, saying, "You've done well to come. You can't remember the lyrics because you don't understand their meaning." He then kindly explained the meaning to Michio, but the explanation was so difficult that, even after hearing it, Michio still didn't understand completely. Even so, Michio was determined to at least remember the meaning this time as they headed home.

There was also *kangeiko*—winter training, where practice took place early in the morning during the coldest part of the year, exposed to the freezing wind. He would play difficult pieces hundreds or even thousands of times. When his hands became too numb from the cold, he would dip them into a basin of icy water before continuing to play until, finally, his fingers bled from the effort.

The winter training continued in this way for almost a month. It was very physically demanding, but Michio persevered until the end.

Caption:
Michio continues practicing the *koto* while enduring the bitter cold.

P10-11

Full Mastery of His Craft

Thanks to his rigorous training, Michio's skills improved rapidly. However, misfortune struck once again.

In 1905, when Michio was 11 years old, his father, Kunijirō, left the company where he had been working and started his own business. However, the business failed and Kunijirō took his family to Korea (now South Korea) to run a small shop, leaving Michio and his grandmother behind in Japan. Unfortunately, the family was caught up in a violent uprising, during which all their goods were stolen, and Michio's father was severely injured, leaving him unable to work. As a result, he could no longer send money to Michio.

Michio and his grandmother went to his master for advice. Sympathizing with their situation, the master offered Michio a position as his assistant which would provide him with an income. However, to become an assistant, Michio first needed to earn his full master's license (*menkyo kaiden*), which required a large payment as a form of gratitude. Naturally, Michio had no way to pay such a sum and was deeply troubled. Sensing the child was worried, the master spoke to Michio in a low voice, "I know you cannot afford the payment because of your family's circumstances and you must feel bad about it in front of everyone else. I will cover the cost for you and you can hand it in with the others as if you brought it yourself."

Michio was so overwhelmed by the master's kindness that he couldn't find the words to thank him and his tears flowed uncontrollably. Later, Michio recalled, "I can never forget how grateful I felt for my master's kindness." In 1905, having officially earned "full mastery of his art", Michio was granted permission to use the character "Naka" from his master's name, "Nakajima", and he took on the professional name "Nakasuga Michio".

Caption:
Michio sobs uncontrollably as his master offers to cover the cost required for his master's license.

P12-13

To Korea

One day, Michio's father, whose injuries had still not healed, visited him from Korea.

"I really need your help, Michio," he said.

Michio had finally just about managed to make a living for himself, but now he had to travel to Korea to support his family. Although he was still in training and had not yet learned all the *koto* pieces, he left his beloved master and set off for the distant and unknown land of Korea. It was the summer of Michio's 13th year.

In September, 1907, Michio and his grandmother moved to Jinsen (now Incheon), a port town about 45 kilometers west of Keijō (now Seoul). The family's home was very small, with only two rooms—one about six *tatami* mats in size, and the other four and a half mats. During the day, Michio taught *koto* to female students and at night, he gave *shakuhachi* lessons to older men, despite having only ever learned to play the instrument by himself. With this work, Michio supported his family.

Michio also wished to continue his own studies, so he had to wake up early to practice *koto* by himself while the others were still sleeping. No doubt as a result of this, by the evening he was so tired that he often fell asleep as he taught *shakuhachi*. Eventually, his students became angry and stopped coming and there were even times that Michio had to go with his father to apologize to them.

However, as a young boy, no matter how hard he worked teaching the *koto* and *shakuhachi*, he was unable to earn enough to fully support his family. The most painful thing during this time was hearing his father having to apologize to debt collectors. Still, perhaps because of the poverty, it is said that they all became closer and were more like a family as they suffered together.

Caption:
Michio falls asleep in front of his student while teaching *shakuhachi*.

P14-15

His First Composition, "Transformations of Water"

After moving to Korea, unfortunately, Michio had no one to teach him and could only practice the songs he had already learned. This left him feeling unsatisfied and he began to think about composing his own music.

One day, Michio heard his younger brother Keiji, who was in second year of higher elementary school (equivalent to sixth grade of elementary school today), reading "*Mizu no Hentai*" ("Transformations of Water") from a textbook and he was immediately drawn to it. The text was a series of seven traditional *waka* poems that described the ever-changing nature of water, from mist to clouds, rain, snow, hail, dew and frost.

The sound of drops falling from the eaves of the old house where Michio lived, the rhythmic patter of raindrops hitting the tin roof, the sound of rain turning to snow, the noise that hail makes, and the soft dripping of melting snow. Michio had always listened intently to these sounds and now he was able to experience the wonders of nature expressed in "Transformations of Water" as his younger brother read the poems.

"I really want to put these words to music," Michio thought.

From then on, he worked every day on his composition, playing and revising, playing and revising until, after about 30 days, he finally had something he was satisfied with. He enjoyed the days spent developing musical ideas and the challenge of writing a piece of music. This was the start of Michio's deep fascination with composing.

This work became his first composition and is the most outstanding among the more than 400 pieces he would later create-"Transformations of Water".

Composed in 1909 when Michio was just 14 years old, this significant piece takes about 17 minutes to play and added an important chapter to the history of Japanese music.

In the summer of that same year, the Korean Resident-General at the time, Itō Hirobumi, visited Jinsen and heard Michio perform "Transformations of Water". Itō was very impressed and praised him, saying, "This is remarkable, especially for someone so young. I will certainly take you back to Tokyo." However, just over three months later, Itō was assassinated at Harbin Station, and with that, Michio's hopes were scattered like mist, vanishing as the morning dew.

Caption:
Images of "Transformations of Water" spread through Michio's mind.

From Nakasuga to Miyagi

In 1910, a year after completing "Transformations of Water", Michio's grandmother, who had always taken care of him, died after catching a cold. About the same time, his father began working for a local government, so Michio had to leave his family and went to live with one of his students, Konishi Masu, and her husband in the central city of Keijō. The Konishis had been financially supporting the Suga family for some time.

As the talented young *koto* player Nakasuga Michio became increasingly famous, he was even invited to perform in front of Queen Yi, and the number of his students increased, providing him a little more financial security.

Feeling that he wanted to study more, Michio, accompanied by his younger brother Keiji, traveled to Japan in July, 1911 to visit his old teacher, Nakajima *Kengyō*. They stayed for about a month, learning pieces he hadn't yet mastered, making use of Keiji's junior high school summer vacation for the trip.

Eventually, the Konishis, having agreed to pay for Keiji's education and living expenses, made a proposal to Michio's father. They suggested Michio marry Kita Nakako, a widow who was related to Mrs. Konishi and also a performer of *koto* and *jiuta* (a style of *shamisen* music). They asked that Michio be adopted into Nakako's family by marriage in order to revive her family's name of "Miyagi", which at that time had ceased to exist as there were no heirs, and so Michio married Nakako, taking on the name "Miyagi Michio".

From December 28,1913, Michio and Nakako went on a 70-day study trip across Japan. In Kobe, he was able to hear a performance by Nagatani Yukiteru *Daikengyō*, a master of *jiuta shamisen* from Kumamoto, and the trip proved to be very fruitful for Michio.

In this way, Michio continued to train in Japanese classical music even during his time in Korea. When he later released his own compositions in Japan, some people criticized him, saying he didn't understand classical music, but in reality, he loved classical music deeply and devoted himself to its study throughout his life.

Caption:
Michio and Nakako listen intently to a *jiuta shamisen* performance by Nagatani Yukiteru *Daikengyō*.

Encounters On The Way To Tokyo

In 1916, at the young age of 22, Michio rose to the highest rank in the *koto* and *jiuta* world of "*Daikengyō*", making him, in both name and reality, the undisputed leader in the world of *koto* music in Korea. However, Michio wasn't satisfied with that. He aspired to do all he could to move to Tokyo, present his own compositions to the wider world and aim to also be the best in Japan. Along the way, he would meet various people who were to support him in this quest.

One of these encounters was with the *shakuhachi* player, Yoshida Seifū , who he met in Keijō in June, 1914 and who would later become Michio's key collaborator in developing "The New Japan Music Movement". After the Meiji era, it became common for *koto* music to be performed in ensemble with the *shakuhachi*. In September of the following year, Seifū, who was 3 years older than Michio, left for Tokyo, saying, "I will return to get you when the time is right."

In October of that same year, Michio also met Nakao Tozan , the founder of the Tozan school of *shakuhachi* . The following year, when Tozan came back to Keijō, he was struck by the originality of Michio's composition for *koto* and *shamisen* quartet entitled "*Karaginuta*", and was also very impressed by Michio's *shamisen* skills.

A month later, this time Kawase Junsuke , a leading figure in the Kinko school of *shakuhachi*, and his wife, Satoko , who was a principal student of Nagatani *Daikengyō* (see P17), and also a major influence on the world of *koto* and *jiuta* music in Tokyo, both recognized Michio's talent and encouraged him to move to Tokyo.

As if putting the final touches to his preparations for the big step to Tokyo, Michio headed to Kumamoto to practice under Nagatani *Daikengyō* from December 26. During this time, he also received a letter from Seifū once more urging him to move to Tokyo and in February, 1917, just before spring, Michio finally left Korea, where he had spent the last 10 years of his life.

Caption:
Yoshida Seifū plays the *shakuhachi* while Michio plays the *shamisen*.

The Impact of His First Recital

In April 1917, when Michio stepped onto the platform at Tokyo Station, he was relieved to hear Yoshida Seifū's loud voice calling out, "You made it!"

Seifū initially provided accommodation for Michio in one of his letting properties but later, with the help of the Konishis, he was able to rent a small house of his own and posted a sign outside saying, "*Koto* Professor", but he failed to attract any students. He'd built up a solid reputation for himself in Korea, but here in Tokyo, he was simply an unknown newcomer.

It was Michio's first Tokyo recital, held at the Central Hall in Hongo in May, 1919, that initially drew attention to him. This was when he was 25 years old, 2 years after he had arrived at Tokyo Station.

His life in Tokyo up until the recital had been absolutely wretched, with living in poverty and the death of his wife Nakako through illness. He was only able to hold the recital due to the initial support of Yoshida Seifū and, later, his second wife Sadako, who he had married in 1918.

This first recital featured a total of 11pieces. All of the pieces, such as "*Mizu no Hentai*" ("Transformations of Water") and "*Karaginuta*", were Michio's original compositions that deviated greatly from the conventional concept of *koto* and *jiuta* music.

The reviews of the performance were sharply divided into 2 camps. Western music artists, scholars and literary figures voiced generally favourable opinions, but many traditional Japanese musicians reacted with hostility to Michio's style.

They considered him heretical, saying, "He's destroying the traditions of *koto* music and relying on gimmicks."

They criticized Michio harshly, accusing him of not understanding Japanese classical music.

On the other hand, practitioners of Western music, who wanted to go beyond merely assimilating techniques of that world and were consciously beginning to incorporate elements and methodology of traditional Japanese music into their work, took a keen interest in Michio's compositions.

Caption:
Michio plays the *koto* at his first recital. The Central Hall in Hongo is depicted in the background.

P22-23

The Birth of "New Japan Music"

The following year, on November 27, 1920, Michio held a joint performance of musical pieces with Western-style composer Motoori Nagayo , called the "New Japanese Music Grand Concert".

Motoori is now famous for composing children's songs like "*Nanatsu no Ko*" and "*Akai Kutsu*", but at that time he was aiming not only to write children's songs but also to compose Western music that incorporated elements of traditional Japanese music.

It was in this context that he collaborated with Michio, who was creating traditional Japanese music which incorporated elements and influences of Western music, and the concert was a great success. However, as Motoori gradually shifted to composing primarily children's songs and vocal pieces, he stopped using the term "New Japanese Music."

On the other hand, there appeared in the traditional Japanese music world a number of others who began to follow Michio's path. However, their works could no longer be categorized under the existing genres such as *koto*, *jiuta* or *shakuhachi* music. Therefore, when these works were presented in broadcasts, recordings and concert programs, they were classified under the name "New Japanese Music." Over time, this name became established as a historical term, referring to the musical movement centered around Michio that aimed to modernize traditional Japanese music during the Taisho and early Showa periods, as well as the works created within that movement.

The particular musical characteristic of people in this movement was that they composed pieces for traditional Japanese instruments with an awareness of Western music. In other words, they aimed to create a new kind of music that reflected the times by introducing Western elements into classical Japanese music.

Caption:
Motoori Nagayo stands before a background of the sun setting between the mountains as crows fly in the evening sky. In the foreground stands Miyagi Michio, whose aim was to reform Japanese traditional music.

P24-25

Fusion of Japan and the West

Michio grew up listening to Western music in the Kobe foreign settlement during his childhood and his interest in Western music grew even stronger through hearing Japanese military bands stationed in Korea and listening to records played to him by a group of Greek friends of his. However, it was not until he came to Tokyo in 1917 that he began to seriously study Western music. He attended lectures by musicologist Tanabe Hisao and went to concerts by top international performers visiting Japan, such as cellist Bogumil Sykora and violinist Jascha Heifetz .

Michio also ordered Braille scores* of Western music from abroad for study and, as he himself said, "Records are my teachers," using them, too, as a learning resource. Through self-study, he incorporated elements of Western music into his compositions for traditional Japanese music.

His famous piece "*Haru no Umi*" ("The Sea in Spring") is

written in the Western ternary form of A-B-A'. The beautiful and easy-to-remember melody and rhythm are Western and are quite different to the melodies and rhythm of traditional *koto* and *jiuta* music. At the same time, the piece uses traditional Japanese scales, giving it a distinctly Japanese feel. This allows the piece to sound Japanese even when played on Western instruments, like the piano or flute, and it is often cited by modern Japanese people as a foremost representative example of Japanese music. Furthermore, it is a piece that foreigners can also easily appreciate as Japanese music.

On the other hand, his debut piece "*Mizu no Hentai*" ("Transformations of Water") is strictly traditional in scale, form, melody and rhythm, but it is the fundamental creative and compositional attitude at its heart that was innovative. Whereas traditional *koto* music relied on combining conventional musical forms and melodies, resulting in abstract, emotionally subdued pieces, "Transformations of Water" is unique in its abundant use of original musical forms and melodies in an effort to vividly depict natural scenes. This focus on individuality in composition was different to traditional Japanese music and was, so to speak, more in line with the modern compositional attitudes of Western music, which is why it is so highly regarded today.

Musical notation in which the pitch, duration, etc. are represented by a combination of six raised dots so that they can be felt by the touch of the fingertips.

Caption:
With a Braille score in the background, Michio is pictured listening to a record and a visiting musician plays the violin.

P26-27
Depicting the Heart: "*Haru no Umi*" ("The Sea in Spring")

"*Haru no Umi*" ("The Sea in Spring") was written at the end of 1929, inspired by the theme of the following year's New Year Imperial Poetry Gathering, "Rocks By The Sea". It premiered on January 2, 1930 on the Hiroshima Broadcasting Station. While the piece is now his most famous work, it did not initially receive much attention upon its release.

What propelled it to fame was his performance of the piece with the female French violinist Renée Chemet. After visiting Michio to hear him play Japanese music, Chemet was so captured by "The Sea in Spring" that she arranged the *shakuhachi* part herself for violin and performed it with Michio at the "Chemet Farewell Concert" on May 31,1932. Their performance was highly praised and the pair later recorded the same piece, with the record being released in Japan, France and America to much acclaim. This led to the name "Miyagi Michio" becoming well-known throughout the world.

Later, Michio explained in an essay where his motivation to write the piece came from, "One time, I was traveling by boat through the Seto Inland Sea and I was deeply struck by the tranquil atmosphere of the sea in spring." Michio often found inspiration for his music in nature. One of the defining characteristics of his music is its ability to describe scenes, but not by just depicting sounds literally, like onomatopoeia or mimicry. Instead, it expresses musically the vague impressions and emotions that the scene stirred in his heart. Though Michio was blind, when we listen to his music, we can vividly picture the scene he had in his mind when he wrote it. This ability to convey mental images through sound is also found in the works of the French composers Ravel and Debussy, both of whom Michio greatly admired. The calm, flowing melodies of "The Sea in Spring" are the reflection of the peaceful image he had in his mind of the spring sea, and it is this portrayal of such emotions that allows the piece to appeal so directly to people's hearts.

Caption:
Michio performs "The Sea in Spring" with the French violinist Renée Chemet. An image of the spring sea is depicted in the background.

P28-29
Essays and Music

When people think of Miyagi Michio, they tend to imagine he must have been a gloomy person as he was blind, was separated from his mother at an early age and grew up in extreme poverty, but his true face was full of humanity. The real Michio was a very warm and energetic person. He loved being in lively company, enjoyed telling jokes and was very afraid of thunderstorms. His playful and cheerful personality can also be glimpsed in his essays.

In 1935, at the suggestion of his close friend and essayist Uchida Hyakken, he published his first collection of essays titled "*Nenbutsu in the Rain*". He would go on to publish a further seven collections in his lifetime, which were highly praised by leading literary figures, including Kawabata Yasunari and Murō Saisei.

Although these are essays written by a man who had achieved fame and success as a musician, they do not contain the anecdotes and grandiose artistic discussions that you might expect from such a master. Instead, he writes cheerfully about his own failures. His writings express his gratitude to those around him and his love for nature and his own characteristically witty expressions can be seen throughout. Even when he talks about sad or difficult experiences, his writing remains calm and composed, which makes it even more moving for the reader.

His memories from his childhood when he could still see are described vividly, with many visual details, but after losing his sight, visual descriptions disappear completely. However, it is from this point on that Michio's unique world begins to appear through his sharp sensitivity and singular perspective. He created his own particular literary style by using all of his senses, including hearing and touch, to deeply feel and express the wonders of nature. This expression in his writing of Michio's heightened sensibility after having lost his sight can also be seen in his music, particularly in his many pieces on the theme of nature, such as "Transformations of Water" and "The Sea in Spring".

Caption:
Michio writes an essay on a Braille typewriter.

P30-31

Development of New Instruments

In order to create a new style of music, Michio also developed new instruments.

The first of these was the "17-string *koto*", introduced at a concert in October, 1921. This instrument is a large *koto* designed to produce lower tones, and it has since become firmly established as a standard Japanese musical instrument, with many composers still creating pieces using it today.

Around 1925, Miyagi expanded on the conventional *kokyū* and developed a larger *kokyū* with greater volume and an extended range that included lower tones. This instrument is known today as the "large *kokyū*" or "Miyagi *kokyū*" (see P33).

Then, at a concert in November, 1929, he unveiled the "80-string" *koto*, shaped somewhat like a grand piano. The design of this instrument attempted to expand the acoustic range of the *koto* while preserving its unique tone and characteristics. However, because the body of the *koto*, which acted as a soundboard, was too small to fully accommodate all 80 strings, it wasn't successful acoustically and was eventually destroyed during the war. From around 1955, various *koto* musicians went on to develop the "30-string", the "25-string" and the "20-string" *kotos*, but Michio's 80-string *koto* can be considered to have paved the way for all these later multi-stringed instruments.

Also, in an attempt to simplify and popularize the *koto*, Michio made the "*Tan-goto* (short *koto*)" which was about two thirds the size of a conventional *koto* and made use of screws which allowed even amateurs to easily tighten the strings. This instrument, unlike his others, was designed specifically for use in schools.

As this shows, Michio was also enthusiastic about education.

Caption:
Michio plays the 80-string *koto*, which was the size of a grand piano.

P32-33

Reform of Teaching Methods and Children's Songs

One teaching method of Michio's that differed greatly from traditional styles was his active use of sheet music. Previously, music was taught without written scores, so students spent a lot of time memorizing pieces. Michio, however, used sheet music to streamline his teaching methods, allowing him to focus more on teaching technique and musical composition. Michio himself understood the convenience of sheet music well, as he had learned Braille notation at age 14 or 15 and had used Braille sheet music from very soon after.

In August, 1930, Michio offered a *koto* music class over the radio, which was very well received. For that reason, the radio lessons were repeated several times and a textbook was produced for each broadcast. These texts later became the basis for a comprehensive instructional book called "*The Miyagi Michio Collection of Short Pieces*" which was designed to allow even complete beginners to learn the techniques of *koto* and *jiuta* performance. The short pieces gradually increased in difficulty from songs without lyrics to those including lyrics and to facilitate this, "*dōkyoku*", children's songs, were used. These "*dōkyoku*" are *koto* pieces for children that Michio created with the children's song poet Kuzuhara Shigeru when he first moved to Tokyo. This may have been influenced by his own struggles memorizing lyrics as a child.

By its nature, teaching is rather inconspicuous work which doesn't leave a lasting legacy like compositions do or attract the attention one receives through performance. On top of that, it doesn't produce "effects". Nonetheless, Michio was determined to put all his efforts into this quiet work. Furthermore, in his "*dōkyoku*", he ingeniously imitated the cries of animals, such as cats and dogs, on the *kokyū*, making the music fun to listen to and causing it to become very popular on records and at concerts. This helped to increase the number of people playing the *koto*.

Caption:
    Behind a child singing children's songs, a woman plays the *koto* and Michio plays the large *kokyū*. In the background is an image of the book "*The Miyagi Michio Collection of Short Pieces*".

P34-35

Reviving Classical Music in a Modern Performance

In his performances, Michio also broke new ground, modernizing Japanese music and bringing classical pieces from the Edo period into the present.

Originally, *koto* and *jiuta* music was performed in a *tatami* mat room at home, or other such small spaces, for one's own education or entertainment. However, with the influence of Western music, concerts purely for the appreciation of the music itself began to appear and the location for such performances moved from the home to large concerts halls. Michio developed new performance methods to suit these larger spaces.

First of all, in terms of instruments, Michio played the plain *koto* with a pure, unadorned sound used by followers of the Yamada School of *koto* music, despite coming from the Ikuta School himself. He made innovative adjustments to the instrument, such as thinning the *koto* picks and using narrower strings, which led to a performance with a beautiful tone which was delicate yet had a powerful core and that resonated even in large halls.

As for performance, Michio created a propulsive style that emphasized the flow of the music. This did not mean simply increasing the tempo.

His energetic performance captivated audiences by taking the dynamics and phrasing inherent in the music and expressing it freely, in contrast to the more restrained style found in conventional classical music performances.

One Western music composer said, "Though the music is old-fashioned and classical, Miyagi's performance appeals to a modern audience with his precise expression that rediscovers the beauty in traditional music."

Caption:
    A close-up of Michio's hands playing the *koto*.

P36-37

New Musical Styles For Large Ensembles

Michio also wrote new-style pieces for large vocal groups and large ensembles of traditional Japanese instruments.

Usually, the largest ensemble used to present *koto* and *jiuta* music was a chorus and a 3-piece instrumental group consisting of a *koto*, a *shamisen* and either a *shakuhachi* or *kokyū*, but Michio composed arrangements for larger ensembles.

These pieces didn't just make use of the 17-string *koto*, that Michio himself had created, to support the lower tones and the large *kokyū* to provide the melody, he wrote arrangements for choral and large ensembles of both Eastern and Western instruments, including instruments from *gagaku* (court music), such as the *shō* (a wind instrument), the *kakko* (an hourglass drum) and the *gakudaiko* (a large, hanging drum), also the *kotsuzumi* (a drum used in *hayashi*, a musical group for festivals and traditional dance performances), and even the flute, all in order to produce his desired tones.

Traditionally, different genres of classical Japanese music, such as *gagaku*, *nagauta* (singing accompanied by the *shamisen*) and *noh* theatre, each had their own specific instruments. The *shō* and the *kakko* were only used in *gagaku*, while the *shamisen* was never used in *gagaku* or *noh*. However, Michio broke down these barriers and used instruments freely to create new music with new ensembles never before seen in the Japanese music world. When composing, he already had a musical image in mind and used any instruments necessary to create the tones he wanted.

He also collaborated with Western composers to create four concertos for *koto* and Western orchestra, beginning with "Variations on *Etenraku*," a piece commissioned in 1928 to celebrate Emperor Showa's enthronement. Many of these large ensemble pieces were commissioned by Tokyo Music School (now the Faculty of Music, Tokyo University of the Arts), where Michio taught, which shows how highly regarded this type of music was at the time.

Caption:
    A concerto being performed by *koto* and a full orchestra.

P38-39

Sudden Death and Eternal Life

After the end of World War II, Michio's popularity continued to grow. In February, 1946, just six months after the end of the war, he received many commissions to create music, beginning with *kabuki*, movies and dance performances. In addition, as commercial broadcasting stations opened after the war, his radio appearances increased and he became extremely busy, hosting regular programs, performing in concerts nationwide and teaching lessons at Tokyo University of the Arts.

During this time, Michio was asked to travel to Europe to represent Japan at conferences and concerts organized by the International Folk Music Council (now the International Council for Traditional Music). In the summer of 1953, Michio embarked on a 43-day concert tour and returned to Japan having achieved great success, including taking first prize at a concert in Pamplona, Spain.

On June 24, 1956, Michio was aboard the sleeper express "*Ginga*" with his niece, Kiyoko, headed out on a trip to perform "Variations on *Etenraku*" with the Kansai Symphony Orchestra. The tour would take them to Osaka, Kobe and Kyoto and he must have been excited about the prospect of these large-scale concerts accompanied by a full orchestra taking place across the Kansai region. As the train set off, Michio began reading and, as was his usual habit, chatted with Kiyoko while drinking a glass of *sake*. He had Kiyoko lead him to the restroom twice and, around 11p.m. she reminded him to wake her if he needed the restroom again and she retired to sleep.

However, in the early hours of the next morning, June 25, Michio was discovered below a railway bridge about 500 meters east of Kariya Station, having fallen from the train. As a station worker took him to the hospital, he asked, "Where is this place?" and, though he received treatment, he gradually lost consciousness and, at 7:15a.m. at the height of his popularity, Michio passed away aged 62, in a hospital room surrounded by strangers, far from home.

NHK broadcast the sad news on that morning's bulletin and the evening newspapers reported it widely, accompanied by photos of Michio. His sudden death came as a shock to people all over Japan.

However, many of Michio's compositions, lead by "The Sea in Spring", continue to be performed to this day. Moreover, without the instruments he developed and the compositional methods he pioneered, the music scene of Japan today would never have been born. Miyagi Michio will live on forever in the music he created.

Caption:
Miyagi Michio and the sleeper express "*Ginga*" heading into the light. The picture depicts an image of Michio's music living on forever.